Colby's Not-So-Scary Book About T1D

One Kid's Story of Type 1 Diabetes

The events and conversations in this book have been
written down to the best of the author's ability, although
some names and details have been changed to
protect the privacy of individuals.

Copyright © 2018 Nicole Neeley

All rights reserved. No part of this book may be reproduced
or used in any manner without written permission of the
copyright owner except for the use of quotations in a book review.

First Edition: August 2018

Cover design and illustrations copyright © 2018 Colby Neeley

This book is for the kids and parents
starting out on a T1D journey.
You are not alone.

And it is for Colby,
the hero of our story.

"It's Christmas!" squealed three excited girls jumping from their beds. They couldn't wait to open presents and look inside their stockings!

"He's been sick for months," Colby's mom said. "He won't stop drinking water, and he keeps going to the restroom day and night."

"You're right," his dad agreed. "Everything makes him grumpy, and he cries for no reason. No matter how much he sleeps, he's still tired."

"I'm taking him to Dr. Stanley," Colby's mom said. "We need to know what's making him sick."

A few days later, she made Colby an appointment.

Dr. Stanley was Colby's favorite doctor. He checked Colby's blood and said, "Your blood sugar is too high! You have type 1 diabetes. I'm sending you to the hospital." Colby didn't understand what Dr. Stanley was saying, and that made him nervous.

How to pronounce "Diabetes"

di-e-bee-teez (Correct!)

di-e-be-dus (Not correct)

di-e-be-dis (Not correct)

What is Type 1 Diabetes?
(...or T1D)

Type 1 Diabetes is a disease caused when your body attacks it's own *pancreas*.

Glucose is a type of sugar found in foods like fruit, bread, and milk.

When your body is healthy, your pancreas makes insulin, a *hormone* that turns glucose into energy.

When you have T1D, your pancreas doesn't make its own insulin. So glucose stays in your body and makes you sick.

Colby's dad met them at the hospital. A friendly doctor came in Colby's room.

Hormones are messenger molecules that travel to different parts of your body and help control how your cells and organs do their work.

"Colby, everybody needs insulin to live and be healthy. Insulin is a hormone made in your pancreas. It's a key that unlocks and opens the door to the cells of your body and lets in glucose, a sugar in your blood. Your cells turn glucose into energy. Energy helps you run, play, and do things you enjoy.

But your pancreas isn't working, so you will need to get insulin from **injections**. Injections are another way to say shots," he explained.

The nurse came to see Colby the next day.

"Hi Colby! I'm going to teach you how to use a blood glucose meter to check your sugar and how to give yourself injections. You will do this before each meal and snack," she said.

"Your insulin injection needs to go in the back of your arm, a leg, a hip, or your stomach. Choose a different spot each time, so the skin where you give your injection doesn't get an infection."

After they left the hospital, Colby and his mom headed to Ms. Jen's office. Ms. Jen was a **nutritionist**.

"Good morning," she began. "Today, I will show you how to read nutrition labels to find out the number of carbohydrates in different foods. That helps you decide how much insulin to give yourself."

Ms. Jen showed Colby her kitchen with plastic food and asked, "Do you want to play together?"

"Yes, please!" Colby said.

A nutritionist is a person who studies food and how it works in your body. They are food experts!

Nutrition Facts:
Serving Size: 1 Cup
Servings Per Cont: 15

Calories 150
Total Fat 8g
Cholesterol 35mg
Sodium 125mg
Potassium 390mg
Total Carbohydrate 12g
Dietary Fiber 0g
Sugars 12g
Protein 8g

She taught him to make healthy choices.
"Which is better, Colby, ice cream or fruit? she asked.
"The ice cream!" Colby said.

"Ice cream tastes good," Ms. Jen told him, "but fruit is better for you. Healthy foods give you nutrients you need to stay well and have energy. It's OK to eat sweet snacks sometimes, but choose healthy foods most of the time."

Colby met his **pediatric endocrinologist** for the first time a few weeks later.

"Hi, I'm Dr. Smith," he said. "Step on the scale and I'll measure and weigh you. Then, we'll check your eyes and ears." Then he asked Colby to take off his shoes. "Close your eyes and tell me when I tickle your feet." Colby couldn't stop laughing during the foot exam.

Dr. Smith made sure Colby was getting the right amount of insulin and that he had enough diabetic supplies. "You need to come back every 3 months for check-ups," Dr. Smith told him.

A pediatric endocrinologist is a doctor who treats kids with diseases like type 1 diabetes.

After each appointment, Colby's mom said, "You choose where we eat lunch today."

"El Nacho!" Colby shouted. "It's my favorite restaurant!"

For 2 years, Colby took 7 shots a day to get his insulin.

"Having diabetes is hard! I don't want to do this anymore!" he cried.

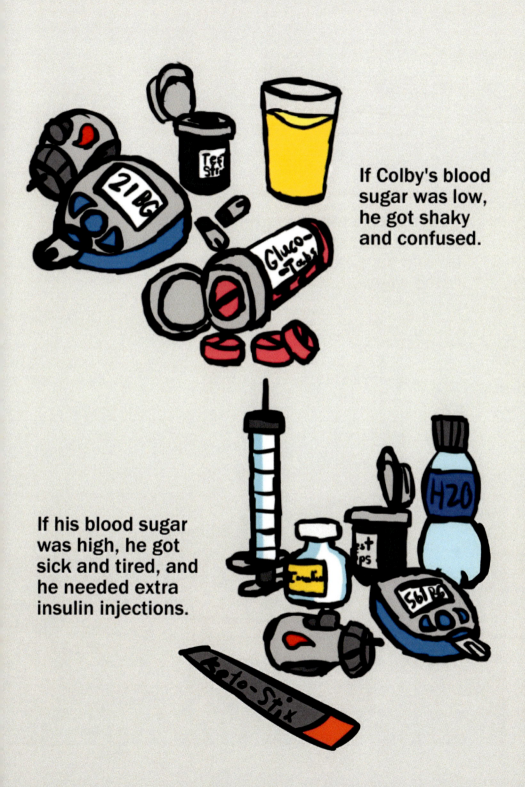

If Colby's blood sugar was low, he got shaky and confused.

If his blood sugar was high, he got sick and tired, and he needed extra insulin injections.

But when his blood sugar was on target, he was full of energy and played outside the whole day. He and his sisters rode bikes, built forts, and hiked in the woods.

One day, Colby's parents got him an insulin pump. A pump trainer explained how it worked.

"The pump has a reservoir, or container, inside to hold insulin. This small tube connects the pump to your body.

Now when you eat, you won't give yourself an injection. Instead, program the pump for how many carbohydrates you will eat and give yourself a **bolus**," she explained.

Colby knew having T1D could be tough.

But having a family and friends to talk to, and a medical team to help him and teach him how to live with **T1D**, made it easier.

Today, Colby is 17 years old. He likes drawing super heroes, writing comic books, and playing with his dog, Jack.

When he grows up, he wants to help other kids with T1D.

Connect with Colby and his family on Facebook at www.facebook.com/t1ddoesnotdefineme.

Challenge Words from the Story:

Type 1 Diabetes - A disease caused when your body attacks its own pancreas and can no longer make insulin.

Hormones - Messenger molecules that travel to different parts of your body and help control how your cells and organs do their work.

Pancreas - An organ in your digestive system that makes juices to help digest your food, and insulin and glucagon to help control glucose in your blood.

Glucose - A type of sugar found in your blood.

Injections - Shots

Nutritionist - A person who studies food and how it works in your body.

Pediatric Endocrinologist - A doctor who treats kids with diseases like type 1 diabetes.

Bolus - The amount of insulin you take through your pump.

Made in the USA
Las Vegas, NV
02 August 2021